JESSE LIVERMORE'S
METHODS OF
TRADING IN STOCKS

The material presented herein derives from a series of inter-
views between Richard D. Wyckoff and Jesse Livermore that
first appeared in "The Magazine of Wall Street" in the 1920s.
The published interviews have been edited and reset by
Martino Publishing into their present form.

RICHARD D. WYCKOFF

Martino Publishing
Mansfield Centre, CT
2014

Martino Publishing
P.O. Box 373,
Mansfield Centre, CT 06250 USA

ISBN   978-1-61427-640-1

Cover design by T. Matarazzo

CONTENTS

"Drifting" Stocks Cost Money
Why He's Always Ready for Opportunities

A Lesson From A Commodity Speculator
A Cool Head For Supreme Decisions
In Summary

CHAPTER 1

Meet the Markets Greatest Trader

Every class in organized society or organized industry has its leaders—its conspicuous figures, who combine in the fullest sense the attributes of their particular class. These leaders are not selected by popular vote. They are not *selected* at all. They reach the highest ranks through their own individual efforts, battling their way against whatever odds appear, redoubling their efforts when the inevitable setbacks occur.

Some of these leaders get there, as the saying goes, more quickly than others; some rise by more brilliant tactics. But, irrespective of how long it takes any of them to arrive, they no sooner definitely do arrive than their fame spreads almost like flashes of light into every nook and cranny of the reading world. An enterprising press, incessantly on the lookout for new idols to set before the public, does the trick.

THE SECRETIVE OPERATOR

The press, which has made the achievements of these leaders common property has, in nearly every case, done the same thing with their methods, their principles and beliefs. To feed the public's insatiable interest in these men's innermost views, their opinions have been demanded on nearly every controversial question under the sun—and in some cases obtained. Scarcely one of them has kept himself to himself, even among the very few who so desired.

There are exceptions to every rule, however; and there is a glaring exception to this one. For the man who towers head and shoulders above all others in one particular field —the man who is almost the sole leader of that field—has successfully evaded publicity in the past, and has kept himself very definitely to himself. This man's reticence has been all the more impressive because of the nature of the field he dominates, one which interests a far greater section of the public than any other, and one in which far greater numbers actively participate. He is the one man in the one field that most people would rather hear talk than anybody else.

The field referred to is that of active speculation in securities. The dominant leader of the field, as everybody knows, is Jesse L. Livermore.

1

A TITANIC OPERATOR

Livermore started trading in securities when he was fourteen years old. He made his first thousand when a mere boy. He has practiced every device known to the active speculator, studied every speculative theory, and dealt in about every active security listed on the New York Stock Exchange.

He has piled up gigantic fortunes from his commitments, lost them, digested, started all over again—and piled up new fortunes.

He has changed his market position in the twinkling of an eye—sold out thousands of shares of long stock, and gone short of thousands of shares more on a decision which required reading only the one word, "but," in a lengthy ticker statement.

If his later experiences were not enough to catch the public fancy, Livermore would have won it by his greatest feat of all: beating the bucket shops.

Beating the cheaters, in fact, was Livermore's pet plan after things had gone against him and he was forced to start anew on a small-lot basis.

HE CONSENTS TO AN INTERVIEW

Until of late, Livermore has maintained absolute silence when questioned about his past operations. Perhaps it was because he did not want to lead the casual, poorly prepared investor into the arena where only master students survived.

It is not his custom to brag about himself, but no doubt he felt that the methods worked out at the cost of a lifetime of battering, courage-straining effort were not lightly to be tossed into the amateur's lap.

Mr. Livermore's willingness to be interviewed by me and to be quoted has been in part influenced by the work I have done in the past in shedding light on Wall Street's ways, Wall Street's men, their theories and methods—in real educational work which has led to more intelligent operating methods being employed by the public.

On the eve of departure for a European vacation, Livermore said, "the most intelligent way to get one's mind attuned to market conditions and to be successful is to make a deep study of industries in order to be able to distinguish the good from the bad; get long of those which are in a promising position and get out of those which are not."

A LESSON TO BE LEARNED

"I regard it of great importance to call the attention of the readers to the above facts, because it has been shown time and again that in Wall Street people very often fail to see the thing that is right under their nose. We now have millions of people interested in the security markets, where there were only thousands in former years; and I cannot emphasize too strongly the importance of the utmost discrimination in the purchase of securities at the present time. One of the greatest mistakes inexperienced investors make is in buying cheap securities just because they are selling at a low price. As a matter of fact, price is not always an indication of cheapness, because non-dividend paying stocks have a certain speculative value that usually causes them to sell at more than they are worth on the basis of either earnings or possible initial dividends. While it may happen that in many instances stocks advance from $30 to $40 a share to over $100, a very much greater proportion of these low-priced stocks have sunk into oblivion by going into receivership, or else they have struggled along striving to make both ends meet for years and years, with only the faintest prospects of ever paying a return to their stockholders.

"In selecting securities, it is only necessary for an investor to determine which industries are in the strongest position, which are less strong and which are comparatively weak, very weak, etc."

AVOID THE WEAK INDUSTRIES

Many investors do not discriminate between strong and weak stocks; and in failing to recognize these essential differences, they place themselves in a position to lose many excellent investment opportunities. As Mr. Livermore says: "I Find it best to avoid the weak industries entirely. I should particularly avoid the lower-priced stocks that have not a firm financial foundation, because when a declining movement does set in, securities representing these weak industries are the first to go and they recover only with the greatest difficulty. Thus, we should avoid getting hung up with these cheap stocks, and companies that are poorly financed, for without ample working capital such concerns will have a hard row to hoe under severe competition.

Just as I would avoid the weak industries and the weak stocks, so I would favor the strongest industries and the strongest stocks. I would choose those industries that face a most promising future so far as can be seen under present conditions. We must, of course, be able and willing to revise our forecasts in the light of developments that come to hand from day to day.

STOCKS HAVE THEIR SEASONS AND FASHIONS

In making selections of securities, investors should remember that the demand does not break out in all commodities at the same time. Everything has its season, and it is very important that this should be taken into consideration. For example, as everyone knows, the best season for the motor and tire stocks is in the spring and summer. The stock market generally discounts this activity a little in advance. I would be illogical to expect these stocks to continue to advance after their best season is over.

Conditions that affect one group of stocks favorably might be precisely the ones to affect others unfavorably.

Thus it will be seen that there are fashions as well as seasons in investments. Conditions change, and one has not only to keep pace with the changes, but to look forward and see what changes are likely to occur six months to a year hence. Unless an investor does this he will soon find himself in the painful position of being hung up with a lot of stocks that have gone over the top and turned downward. He will find his funds tied up so that he can't use them.

Investors should insure themselves against such a situation by not plunging in the cheap stocks, but by keeping the principal portion of their funds liquid so that when a good investment issue comes along they will be in a position to take advantage of it. Perhaps nothing has so interfered with the proverbially poor success of the public in the investment market as this fact—that it does not keep its investment and speculative funds in proper circulation. The public is usually in a loaded-up or tied-up condition. Tell the public that a certain stock may advance a few points a month and do you find them interested? No, they want something that moves more quickly. Yet in a few months they will probably wake up to see the stock selling twenty points higher and the cheap stocks which they bought selling at less than the prices paid for them.

THE ONE SURE WAY TO SUCCEED IN THE MARKET

Tell your readers that there is no magic about success in the stock market. That the only way I know for anyone to succeed in his investments is for him to investigate before he invests; to look before he leaps; to stick to the fundamentals and disregard everything else:

No man can succeed in the market unless he acquires a fundamental knowledge of economics and thoroughly familiarizes himself with conditions of every sort—the financial position of a company, its past history, production, as well as the state of the industry in which it is engaged, and the general economic situation.

LIVERMORE'S ESSENTIAL TO SUCCESS

Essentials to stock market success are knowledge and patience. So few people succeed in the market because they have no patience. They want to get rich quickly. They are not willing to buy when a thing goes down, and wait. They buy mostly when a thing is going up, and near the top.

In the long run, patience counts more than any other element except knowledge. The two really go hand in hand. Those who want to succeed through their investments should learn that simple truth. Also this, investigate before you buy and then you are sure that your position is a sound one. Don't let yourself become discouraged by the fact that your securities are moving slowly. Good securities in time appreciate sufficiently to make it well worthwhile to have patience, especially in a bull market like the present one.

Think in terms of the industrial outlook; choose the strongest company in the strongest industry, and do not buy stocks on hope alone.

The only time to buy is when you *know* they will go up."

CHAPTER 2

How He Prepares for the Day's Work

THE EARLY LIVERMORE

In undertaking to analyze the methods which Jesse L. Livermore employs in the stock market, I shall not begin by presenting the history of his past operations, but will merely recount the fact that he began at an early age (fourteen); and up to 1922 had been trading in stocks for about thirty years. Of this period, twenty-five years were devoted to finding himself. His fortunes during that time fluctuated widely from a five dollar bill to a million dollars, back to nothing and on down to a million or more in debt, all of which showed his ability to make money in the market at times; his difficulty was in keeping it, proving that his methods were then only partly efficient.

How he eventually discovered and conquered his weak points; how he turned his active, uncertain form of trading into comparatively inactive long-pull operating which was consistently profitable in the net, are subjects for later portions of this series. Without further introduction, therefore, let us proceed to analyze Mr. Livermore's methods, for everyone who has attempted to make money in securities is desirous of learning the "how" of the business, and no better example can be found.

ORGANIZING HIS MARKET WORK DAY

An important element in the success of anyone lies in the way his day's work is planned. Comparatively few men plan their business day in advance. They go through a certain routine that varies with the number of callers, conferences or interruptions, leaving them, at the end of the day, with some of the most important matters unexamined, unstudied and undecided. Not so with Livermore. His opinions are based on certain facts. He requires time and seclusion in which to examine, absorb and digest these facts; to form his conclusions and plan his campaigns.

He prepares for his day's work by retiring at ten p.m. He goes to bed early, because he knows that "the adroit man profits by everything, neglects nothing which can increase his chances; the less adroit, by sometimes disregarding a single chance, fail in everything."

IN TRIM FOR THE DAY'S WORK

He desires not only the advantage of plenty of sleep; he wishes to rise early, thoroughly refreshed for the day's work. He puts in an hour or two before breakfast studying world conditions affecting the stock market, banking, foreign trade, money, crops, corporate reports and trade statistics. He chooses the early morning for studying these subjects for at that time his mind is thoroughly rested and cleared of the previous day's impressions, like a photographic plate ready for the negative.

He reads the principal morning newspapers, analyzing and weighing the effect of the news. Most of this has already been developed from world happenings on the previous day, and the greater part has already reached him through the news slips, news tickers and the evening newspapers; but in the morning fresh angles are presented, and these are carefully gone over. He does not follow the common practice of reading the headlines and skimming through the rest of the news. A small item of three lines in an obscure corner of the paper may mean more to him than the entire balance of the contents. He once traveled four thousand miles and took a market position because he had observed a certain brief dividend notice in a newspaper. He has been known to "clean house" to the extent of over 100,000 shares on a single news item and then reverse his position because he found he had misinterpreted it.

DIGS FOR FACTS

The front page spreads and the big headlines in the newspapers he regards as for public consumption. The vital facts, he says, are usually concealed in all sorts of out of the way places. He digs for them. If they cannot be located in the morning or during the day, he will temporarily discard his early-to-bed rule and sit up till one or two in the morning. *He gets what he goes after.*

In certain papers he finds digests of the steel, coal, textile, copper, automobile, equipment, and other leading industries as well as the cotton, grain, sugar and various other commodity markets. All these are scrutinized as indices to conditions in their respective fields. Indirectly they are also guides to correct judgment of business conditions in general.

Anyone who has employed the early hours for such a purpose realizes what an immense advantage is gained in this practice. The house is quiet. Nothing disturbs the flow of thought during a sufficient period for subjects to be taken up, investigated and conclusions reached. No other part of the day affords such a splendid opportunity for the quiet absorption of such data. It cannot so effectively be sandwiched in between tape readings while prices are running out on the ticker during market hours.

There is another advantage which is not so apparent on the surface: these study periods being equally separated by twenty-four-hour intervals, the changes for better or worse are more readily discerned. Mathematicians will tell you that one of the most important factors in studying the curve of any graph showing the progress of an industry, a business, a factor, etc., is *the element of change* toward better or worse, and that these changes should be studied not only with regard to their direction but the speed with which they occur during stated intervals. I have found this true in studying the market at a time when, busily engaged in other fields, I could only devote about an hour a day to the subject. These brief but regular periods proved to be an advantage instead of a disadvantage. Take up any subject under such conditions, and you will find that the effect is like observing a series of photographs taken one week apart showing the progress of a building. One is able to note whether the change in one direction or another be slow or rapid, and as the slowing up of the movement in one direction occurs, he is forewarned that a change is about to take place.

HE LEARNS FOR HIMSELF

Livermore does not concern himself with what this or that person may say about the present condition of a certain industry. He does want to see and study the statistics which show what conditions are likely to prevail in that trade several months from now. When the news items were reporting the steel companies as operating at 25% to 30% of capacity, he told me that the actual figure was less than 20%. That is the kind of information he extracts from various sources, early in the morning, when other people are asleep. His daily concentration on economics, trade tendencies, etc., forms the background for the opinions formed before the market opens at ten a.m.

In a recent discussion Mr. Livermore said: "No man can succeed in the market unless he acquires a fundamental knowledge of economics and thoroughly familiarizes himself with conditions of every sort—the financial position of a company, its past history, production, as well as the state of the industry in which it is engaged, and the general economic situation. There is no magic about success in the stock market. The only way I know for the public to succeed in their investments is for them to investigate before they invest."

He might have added: Get up early in the morning to accomplish this, as there will probably be no time to do it thoroughly during the day, nor at night when the mind is fatigued from the day's activities. More particularly does this apply to those who do not make a business of trading in stocks.

Most people do their thinking in well-worn grooves. They are creatures of habit. They get up at eight because they have to be at the office at nine. In the evening they feel the need of recreation, which often means the theatre, a dancing or bridge party. They consider themselves entitled to such recreation, and if it means being out late, well, they are "good sports and can get along with very little sleep." It is true, they *can* get along, but can they get ahead if they practice it continually?

HE CONCENTRATES ON ESSENTIALS

Contrary to the fixed habits of most men, Livermore is willing to sacrifice many of the so-called diversions which occupy numbers of people from ten p.m. to twelve, one or two, in order that he may devote those few hours to sleep, and thus have his uninterrupted morning period for study. Late hours and late sleep are two things the majority like to indulge in; this majority is known as "the public," millions of whom attempt in a desultory way to master the greatest and most difficult game in the world—one that requires an almost complete reversal of previous mental and physical habits. No one seriously should undertake trading in stocks as a vocation without adopting such methods as will thoroughly equip him for his work. The experiences of Livermore indicate that two of the requisites are: (1) plenty of sleep, and (2) ample time for close and uninterrupted study and reflection on the elements and influences which shape the trend of the market; on the factors which determine prosperity or depression in business in general, and in individual industries and companies in particular.

Livermore is a keen student of human nature in its relation to the stock market. As he himself expressed it in the interview alluded to previously "essentials to stock market success are knowledge and patience. So few people succeed in the market because they have no patience. They want to get rich quickly. They are not willing to buy when a thing goes down and wait. They buy mostly when a thing is going up, and near the top."

Livermore has succeeded because he has made a deep study of the stock market and of himself. That is the way to make a success of anything. Napoleon wrote: "If I appear always ready to meet every emergency, to confront every problem, it is because before undertaking any enterprise I have long considered it and have thus foreseen what could possibly occur. It is no genius which suddenly and secretly reveals what I have to say or do in some circumstance unforeseen by others, it is my own meditation and reflection."

I went into Livermore's office one day with a friend who wanted to give him some facts that had just developed in a certain situation. The friend had barely mentioned the name of the company when Livermore whipped a memorandum out of the top drawer of his desk and said, "is that what you mean? I've had that for days."

THE MARKET REQUIRES STUDY

In an interview some years ago, Mr. Livermore said: "Anyone who figures that his success is dependent upon chance may as well stay out of the market. His attitude is wrong at the very start. The great trouble with the average man who buys securities is that he thinks the market is a gambling proposition.

One should realize at the outset that the work requires the same study and preparation as law or medicine; that certain rules apply to it that are to be studied as closely as if he were a law student preparing for the bar. Many people attribute my success to luck. The fact is, for fifteen years I have studied this subject closely; you might say I have given my life to it, concentrating upon it and putting into it my very best."

CONCLUSION

From the above we learn:

That the attainment of spectacular and permanent success as a stock market operator requires that one devote his life to the business. He should also be possessed of a certain character adapted to this line of work; especially marked abilities in this field, as well as a strong desire to succeed therein.

The average business man who has devoted a good part of his life to other tasks is rarely fitted to become what Wall Street recognizes as an operator, but he can, without interfering with his regular work, acquire an understanding of the business and become a scientific and successful investor in proportion to the effort and the intelligence he puts into the work.

A thorough knowledge of underlying conditions is indispensable.

A certain period of the day should be devoted to study.

Sound opinions may best be formed on the basis of actual facts secured from original and authentic sources. The ability to interpret these facts increases with time and experience.

The real news is not in the headlines. One must seek it elsewhere.

Ability to foresee conditions that will prevail in the future is absolutely essential.

CHAPTER 3

The Special Arrangement of His Office

HOW HE INSULATES HIMSELF FROM BAD INFLUENCES

The environment in which Jesse Livermore does his day's work is one which he has created for himself. It is the out-growth of his long experience in the business of trading in stocks.

Atmosphere is a well known Wall Street term, usually applied to the psychological conditions existing in the Street, but more particularly in the brokerage offices where those who buy and sell securities are accustomed to gather. The atmosphere of the brokerage office varies with the character of the business and the number and average mentality of its clients. There are small offices with a few tickers and other brokerage paraphernalia, a customer's man and a partner or two. It seems like a quiet place, but it is not. A period of fifteen minutes' consecutive thought without interruption is almost impossible. Through all conversation runs the usual line of tips, and gossip exchanges between brokers and clients. Concentration is out of the question unless one possesses the doubtful advantage of being deaf and dumb. In the larger offices, with big quotation boards, audienced by twenty-five or fifty customers, the atmosphere is ten times more tense and more impossible from the standpoint of a professional trader. The little knots around the small, low tickers are sewing circles for gossip. Your neighbor in the next chair always wants to tell you his hopes and fears: what he sees, hears, thinks or knows.

Livermore has been through all this. For a long while he did not enjoy the advantages of silence and seclusion but many years since, he has made a practice of trading from his own private offices where he is not disturbed by the demoralizing hubbub of a customers' room.

The morning journey from his town house or his summer home at Great Neck is made by automobile; he does not use railroad trains or subways. Many wealthy and prominent financiers do so, but they have no special reason for avoiding contact with other people. Livermore has; he knows that if he mixes during the trip to his offices, the subject is bound to turn to the stock market, and he will be obliged to listen to a lot of tips and gossip which interfere with the formation of his own judgment. Playing a lone hand, he does his own thinking and he does not wish to have his mental processes interfered with morning, noon or night.

POISE AND INDISPENSABLE ADJUNCT

One of the most indispensable qualifications to a trader in his position is poise—that state of mental balance which enables him to regard any situation calmly, and from an unbiased point of view, uninfluenced by hopes, or fears. He possesses this desirable characteristic to a most remarkable degree—was evidently born with it and has highly cultivated it since.

WHAT HE HATES THE MOST

Most of all he hates tips. A person with even small experience in Wall Street knows how frequently one will decide to act upon a situation in a certain way, and how readily one is thrown off the course he has mapped out for himself by some insidious suggestion. Having carefully studied out the effect of all these influences he has long since learned that he gets the best results by excluding any element that in the least interferes with the formation of his judgment which is based on the facts, sound reasons and logical conclusions.

Among other practices in his own self-development, he has undertaken a study of psychology. I do not mean that he has merely pondered over the psychological effect of this or that Wall Street phase; he has taken a course—become a student of psychology, just as he has delved into every other factor that will to any degree aid him in his life work. He does not dabble in anything.

HIS OFFICE EQUIPMENT

He arrives at his office, which is on one of the upper floors of a big downtown skyscraper. There is no name on the door. It consists of a reception room, private offices for some of his assistants, and his own private office, separated by swinging doors from his board-room. This is an oblong room with a long silicate quotation board on one side and a row of windows opposite. On the board are exhibited quotations for thirty or forty of the leading active stocks, and a few each of the active futures in cotton, wheat, corn and oats. The quotation board is not arranged according to the ordinary custom prevailing in brokerage houses. The changes in quotations are not posted by means of printed tickets containing merely the opening, high, low and last figures; instead, each stock has its own column running the full length of the board, in which the various changes in quotations are written with chalk, with the numerous sales strung along down below the abbreviations. He prefers this kind of board because it gives him a line on the swings of a stock, the extent of its rallies and reactions, as well as its relative activity. The volume of trading does not appear on the board; he gets this from the tape.

A stock, a cotton, a grain and a news ticker stand in front of the board, several feet away and in the center of it, so that he reads the tape with the light back of him, and he has but to raise his eyes to see any stock on the board.

In many brokerage offices, you see low tickers with bases surmounted by round table tops, and three or four traders gathered about them, some of whom have either to crane their necks or read the tape upside down. Livermore does not believe in low tickers except for use during the brief intervals when he sits down at the desk in his private office. There he has a battery of them. For general use, he wants them tall so that he has to stand up to look at them. He believes that among the many factors that have contributed to his mastery of the business, is the fact that he uses tall tickers, for they keep him on his feet in an erect position so that he can breathe properly and his circulation will be unimpeded. The crouched or lounging position assumed by those who sit around the low tickers, is in direct contrast. He is on his feet practically all day. His telephoning is also done in a standing position. Thus he gets a certain amount of exercise.

SIMILARITY WITH JAMES R. KEENE

With the exception of the quotation board, the chief arrangements in his offices greatly resemble the office of the late James R. Keene, the eminent stock market operator in whose private office it was my privilege to spend many interesting hours. Mr. Keene also used a high ticker and stood on his feet during the market session, stepping back and forth to the telephone a few feet away, or to the booths in the adjoining private office. When not reading the tape—a process in which his piercing eyes seemed to bore into the very vitals of the market—Mr. Keene had a peculiar method of pacing back and forth from the ticker down toward the other end of his office and back, each step taken with a rigidity and a precision, and accompanied by a metronome—like swinging of his clenched fists, expressing a most intense determination.

His tape reading seemed to be done at regular intervals, with a certain number of steps taken as above described, thus apparently dividing his views of the tape into a series of pictures flashed one at a time across his vision, with the short walks serving as periods of digestion of what he had observed. I have previously referred to the value of regularly separated intervals in the study of the market as well as the speed with which these alterations occur.

In the course of our discussion, Mr. Keene would stand facing the ticker, and I on the opposite side. With eye glasses in his right hand, he would emphasize his points; but he would talk just about so long; then his eyes would drop to the tape. Once they fastened on the paper ribbon, I could go on with the conversation but he would not hear a word. His concentration when reading the tape was so complete that all other subjects were completely eliminated. He might step to the phone and ask, "Who's buying that Reading?" or "What's going on in B.R.T.?" Then he would come back and study the tape, take his specified number of paces, finish his mental process, come out of his trance and pick up the conversation where he left off.

In many respects Livermore resembles Keene. Most of all in his eyes, with the lids slightly dropping at the sides, and a similar penetrating quality. His nose, too, is like Keene's—prominent at the bridge. I leave it to experts on physiognomy as to just what that means, but I know that Livermore, like Keene, is deep, sagacious, ingenious, resourceful, self-reliant, far-sighted and possessing lionlike courage. In their methods of operating, too. I find many points of resemblance. Some of these I will explain in chapters to follow.

Very few people can reach Livermore by telephone or in person. He receives some mail, but answers very little. He has no time for correspondence. The market is a man's job. The people he sees and the letters he writes bear a close relation to the market and his operations therein, or he cannot devote the time to them. This is in line with his practice of excluding all non-essentials.

I have already shown that in part, the formation of his judgment grows out of his early morning studies of the fundamentals; but his decisions as to the right stocks and the right time for action are based on what he sees on the tape. The news ticker always plays its part in keeping him in touch with developments as they are flashed along the wires from all parts of the world. He and his assistants keep one eye on the news ticker because a certain report, a paragraph, a line, or sometimes a word will have an important influence on his market position. But he does not merely accept such statements at anything like the face value given them by the public. He endeavors to interpret the real situation disclosed, or the real purpose behind the publication of the items. No one knows better than he that the market is made by and is a reflection of the minds of many men; that some of these men are more powerful than others, that as fellow players in this great game they often endeavor to influence public sentiment as to induce buying or selling by others. He reads between the lines in search of indications as to what "they" are trying to do.

In one of my previous writings, I have described Wall Street as a vast hopper into which, all day long, there pours an unceasing supply of news of every sort—railroad, industrial, corporation earnings, weather reports, items relating to banking, crops, money markets, gold imports, world developments, and thousands of other items bearing upon the stock, bond or commodity markets—all of them influencing to a certain degree the general business situation. Livermore interprets these news items in two ways: first, he judges their direct or indirect bearing on the market or the individual stocks, and next, he observes on the stock ticker the effect of the news—as to how it influences the buying and selling of special stocks for the market as a whole. His own interpretation of a news item may be absolutely opposite from that expressed by the market, but he knows that if the development is of sufficient importance it will, sooner or later, leave its impression on the tape.

He, therefore, endeavors to anticipate the time when other large operators will alter their market positions so as to adjust themselves to the new situation.

If the methods of Jesse Livermore were to be told in two words, they would be these: *He anticipates.*

SUMMARY

From the above we conclude:

That silence and seclusion are essential to the formation of sound, clear and independent judgement. As in any other line of work, one must concentrate. Thinking, planning and execution of business in this field can best be accomplished away from your broker's office.

One requisite is poise.

A knowledge of psychology is an important adjunct to an operator's mental equipment.

Clear-headedness grows out of a good physical condition and a certain amount of exercise is necessary thereto.

Insight, combined with a shrewd interpretation of the news, is absolutely essential, for large events sometimes hang upon small news items.

The effect of the news is an index to the character of the market, the attitude of large interests and their buying and selling.

Speculation, in its truest sense, calls for anticipation.

The tape reflects the operations and motives of large operators and insiders.

The big money is in the long swings.

CHAPTER 4

How Livermore Reads the Tape

With a background of the fundamental position and a clear idea of the long trend of the market, Livermore picks up the tape at the opening of the market for confirmation or contradiction of his previously formed opinion. He has made a certain diagnosis of the present situation and a mental forecast as to what market action is likely. He realizes that the results of the day's trading may alter, to some extent, his opinion as to the future course of prices—supply evidence as to whether his judgment has been right or wrong. If it is right, he sticks; if wrong, he alters his position.

That little, narrow bit of paper ribbon records the hopes, fears and aspirations of millions of people. It is the concrete expression of the minds of all those who buy and sell stocks and bonds. Between four hundred and five hundred of the leading stocks are there recorded in varying quantities and at all sorts of rapidly fluctuating prices. To extract the essence of the market intelligence expressed on the tape is a task which can be accomplished successfully only by one who has a very deep understanding of the business, combined with long training and experience.

Everyone familiar with Wall St. knows that the stock market does not drift about aimlessly, even though it does reflect the attitude of many people, for the public is unorganized and few of those who participate in the great game know what their neighbors are doing. But the large interests and the leading operators have a very clear idea of what they believe certain stocks should sell at or can be made to sell at, and their efforts to induce buying or selling or inactivity at certain levels are problems for the tape reader to solve.

Livermore judges the probable future course of the market and of various stocks by their own action, for this is more significant to him than what any insider says, prints, or promises. He knows that very often insiders are the worst judges of their own stocks, because they know too much about their companies; they are too close to them to see the weak spots; they are often ignorant of technical considerations. In referring to the bullish interviews which occasionally emanate from certain quarters, he has remarked to me what I very well know: that important selling could be traced to the almost identical sources at about the same time. That is one reason why the tape means so much to him, for it shows the real purpose behind the bit of propaganda skillfully press-agented for public consumption.

The tape is a moving picture with no two flashes alike. The picture changes about every two seconds. Each alteration bears a certain relation to what has passed and casts the shadow of what is coming. To read and mentally assimilate these stock market flashes and apply rapid fire horse-sense to them continuously through a five-hour session; to extract the essential facts and sense the purpose and probable outcome of what is happening, is his daily job.

These are some of the things he looks for on the tape: whether opening prices are above or below the previous closing; which stocks are showing weakness or strength at the opening; which are neglected; character of the leadership; which groups (industries) are strongest and weakest; whether former leaders are hesitating and which others are coming to the fore; the power of the strongest or weakest groups to act as a stimulus or to retard the rest of the market; nature of the manipulation; which pools are most active and how their stocks respond to the general or specific news affecting them; probable meaning of this weakness or that strength; volume of trading in the whole market; whether it is increasing or decreasing compared with yesterday, last week, last month; the way in which leaders and secondary leaders respond to stimulation or pressure; nature of the buying or selling, whether mostly manipulative, professional or public; swiftness or sluggishness of the advances or declines and the frequency with which these occur; which lasts the longest; their distance apart; how the market and certain stocks act at the points of resistance; its ability to absorb selling or to supply stocks; whether the principal pools are accumulating, marking up or distributing; whether there is evidence of very much inside operating; whether it is heavy or light; what the floor traders are doing; general position of these professionals—long or short, light or extended; character of the securities being absorbed or liquidated by the public; influences to which they respond; ability of the market to sustain itself without artificial stimulation or pressure; how it acts when left to itself; changes in its condition when the bulls suddenly abandon their tactics; which stock in a certain industry is acting the best or the worst; are insiders taking their time or trying to force a certain situation; whether certain stocks go up easily or whether they show a lack of supporting orders and therefore break badly under a little pressure; whether insiders are buying openly or under cover— cautiously or boldly; and why; when the small or large swings run their courses; relative position of the market today compared with previous days, months and years; where the point of danger lies; which issues have stopped going with the trend or have begun a reverse movement; and—most important of all—when it is time to act in a big or small way.

These are a few of the main considerations which help to form his judgment as to whether his present or contemplated commitments are right or wrong; whether he should maintain his position, flop to the other side or get out of the market altogether. Long practice at the business has put so keen an edge on his judgment that it is almost intuitive. He expects the tape to tell him what is going to happen far in advance of the event, for what is known to one or more persons operating in the stock market is more or less certain to be indicated by their own transactions or those growing out of the situation thus disclosed. He knows that the first thing a person does when he discovers something which may alter the value of certain securities, is not to print it on a news ticker but to buy or sell the stock himself, and then tell his friends about it. That is one kind of "news" Livermore looks for on the tape in his continuous study of the action of the market.

The psychological condition of the Street, meaning the reaction taking place in the minds of the public, as a result of various developments that come to hand from hour to hour, has a very tangible effect upon the market. No one who is operating in a large or small way, or is attempting to float securities or accumulate them, can afford to ignore this highly potent factor, and its effect upon supply and demand.

Some large interest may be attempting to buy 50,000 shares of a certain stock, and the attitude of the public or numerous investors is such that the latter are induced to liquidate their holdings. The selling of, say, 55,000 shares from this source would be sufficient to nullify the effect of the large interests' accumulation and the market would consequently decline instead of advance. From this it will be seen why the psychological conditions are so important, for no one can anticipate the effect of any special developments on the public mind. Judging these conditions—anticipating the probable effect of them, is one of Livermore's strong points.

It would be an error to say that he is not concerned with the small intermediate swings, for he is deeply interested in every kind of a movement that appears on the tape.

He carefully observes the development of the swings running from five to twenty points and occupying periods of from a week to sixty days, and he studies intently the two, three and five-point dips and rallies, for all of these play their part in forming that vast stream known as the stock market which, though frequently altering its course, follows the line of least resistance until its journey upward or downward is ended.

Just as the panics announce to him that it is time to cover and go long, so the topmost section of bull markets exhibit earmarks which a practiced eye may discern. He watches for these because he endeavors to see them before anyone else, and particularly in advance of the pools and other large operators whose strategy he undertakes to solve.

Having accumulated his line at what he believes to be the turning point in a great decline, he is likely to carry the bulk of it for many months, sometimes over a year, because he realizes that it requires a considerable time for general business to recover, earning power to be restored, and increased dividends paid. Therefore, prices of stocks unless artificially stimulated cannot travel their full course in a few months. Being intimately acquainted with all the booms and panics that have occurred during more than a quarter of a century, he possesses what might be known as an educated perspective. Hence, while other people are saying the country is going to the dogs, and emphasizing their opinions by closing out or selling short, he watches carefully for what he terms the psychological buying moment. In the panic of 1907 he spotted it to the very hour. In the depression of 1921 he covered and went long while the market was in its very lowest stages, his published reason being that while there had been an oversupply of goods and commodities, there was likely to be a shortage of goods in the future. But I suspect that his finely-developed sixth sense or intuition told him the exact point in the market when his purchases could best be made.

Every little thing that happens means much at such a time—the pounding by the bears, the public liquidation, the hopeless trade reports, the blue tint of the newspapers, speak volumes. But what he is most deeply interested in is the way in which the selling is absorbed—the resistance which it encounters at different levels; the volume of trading, the hysterical efforts of the various interests who are trying to depress prices; the tactics they use, and the lies they tell. Each factor has its weight, especially at this particular stage of the game.

And it is a game, the greatest in the world, played by millionaires whose knowledge, power and resources are employed in the anticipation of the worldwide changes in conditions that govern the main swings in the prices of securities from low to high and back again. Knowing that any one or set of individuals, no matter how rich or how powerful, is only partly intelligent, he strives to discern the concrete expression of all those millions of minds.

HOW HE JUDGES THE TURNING POINTS

Judging the main turning points in the long swings is the most important thing that he does, and if he could accomplish nothing else in between the panics and booms and accurately judge the right time for changing his position, he knows that he has a starting point for the rolling up of tremendous profits during the intervening year or two while the market is on its way from nadir to zenith. It is perfectly clear why this is so. A man who loads up at the low point of a panic has a certain amount of working capital. If he succeeds in selling out near the top of the boom, he has not only his original capital but his aggregate profits as well. If he then takes a short position with his line increased by reason of these profits and successfully rides this short line down to the next panic, he will find his resources vastly increased.

These lines of stocks which Livermore takes on at the low points are not, of course, always sold at the topmost prices. As the market executes its series of intermediate swings and begins to approach the level when an important turning point is likely to occur, he looks for more frequent reactions, and, therefore, will very often liquidate all or part of his line on some of the strong bulges which occur in the upper stages of the market, or in what is known as the selling zone. He does not consider it good policy to try and get the last point, for many things can happen which might bring the ultimate turning point nearer than he anticipated. He knows that all stocks do not make their tops simultaneously. Some reach their apex months before the last of them have exhausted their lifting power. The bull forces may be likened to an army which is carrying the defenses of the enemy: it can advance just so far without becoming exhausted and falling back. He knows that the principal bull ammunition is money and that general conditions govern and limit the extent of any move; also that it is not so much the news, the statistics, the dividends, etc. that are important but what is of dominating importance is the effect of the developments on the minds of men and the extent to which traders and investors are thereby induced to buy or sell. The market is not affected by what a million people think about the market, but it is immediately affected by their actual buying and selling or their failure to do either.

HOW HE PLAYS THE INTERMEDIATE SWINGS

While the long swings are of the utmost importance to him, they do not by any means constitute all of his operations. He is an active trader, for long ago he cured himself of jumping in and out of the market day after day. Next in importance to the trades which he makes are the intermediate swings running from ten to thirty points and from a week or two to a few months in duration. Let us say that the market is getting into the upper levels and, although not at the turning point, becomes overbought and the technical position is such that a reaction often to fifteen points is imminent. He decides that under such conditions it is best for him to reduce his line of long stocks in order that he may take advantage of whatever decline occurs by replacing them at lower prices. He may have twenty or thirty points profit in a certain lot of stock which he believes will sell at a higher figure eventually, but if he can close this out on the verge of a sharp reaction and replace it ten points cheaper, he has thereby reduced the original cost by that much.

His judgment of the time and the direction of these intermediate swings can only be formed accurately by the action of the market as recorded on the tape of the ticker. He cannot gauge it properly in any other way. Where else can he see the gradual alteration from strength to weakness in the market; the complete supply of the absorption power; the ultimate weakening of support and the numerous other characteristics of such an episode.

Just as the market displays to his practiced eye the downward phase, so it forecasts the end of the reaction and the time to resume the long side. These indications appear in the leading stocks of important groups and in many individual issues—usually the most popular trading mediums. The principles of judging the market by its own action, Livermore learned long ago and he found that they operate over the whole wide range of stock market movements, from the little half-hourly ripples back and forth to the great swings in prices running from one to three years. It is a question of supply and demand and once recognized and properly applied, it goes a long way toward solving most stock market problems.

The market moves along the line of least resistance and when demand is greater than supply this line is upward. To detect the momentary changes as well as those taking a longer time to work out, is the daily task of Mr. Livermore, just as it is the business of every manufacturer and merchant to judge the future course of his particular industry.

CHAPTER 5

How He Makes His Commitments and Limits His Risk—His Minimum Prospective Profit

It is common practice in Wall Street to buy a stock because some one tells you it is going up, without regard to the relative risk or the size of the anticipated profit. That this is a grave mistake has been proven in thousands of instances during many years of Wall Street history. There were doubtless people who bought New Haven at $250 per share because they either believed or were informed that it was going up. Few of them would have been convinced if some one had told them at the time that they were risking nearly $25,000 for a possible profit of $1,000 or $2,000.

If an operator could trade in stocks without danger of loss there would be no object in endeavoring to ascertain in advance what the size of the profit might be; but so long as losses are inevitable and should be considered as part of the operating expenses, just as commission, revenue tax and interest are operating expenses, the estimated profit becomes a very important factor in successful trading.

It is almost an appalling fact that the practice of the public is to accept a profit of two or three points, but to stand for a loss ranging from ten to thirty points, and sometimes fifty or a hundred points. This means that the public reverses one of the first principles in successful stock trading which is: cut your losses and let your profits run.

LESSONS FROM SUCCESSFUL OPERATORS

Nearly all the successful operators of the past fifty or sixty years have adopted and preached this principle. It was a by-word of Jim Keene's; it was followed by Cammack; it was practised by Dixon G. Watts, who was one of the most successful cotton speculators ever known; it was advocated by E.H. Harriman, who was once a floor trader, and who said: "If you want to be successful in trading, *kill* your losses; try to keep them down to three-eighths of a point but *never* risk more than one point," (Of course, Harriman said this from a floor trader's standpoint; such close trading is not possible to anyone who pays commissions and trades from an office).

25

These great operators also followed the rule of letting their profits run. Many of them pyramided their profits, which is the same thing more intensively applied.

Jesse L. Livermore learned both these rules in bucket shops, where in his earlier years he learned how to trade. In these establishments only two points margin were required, and, when this slender margin was wiped out, he had documentary evidence that his judgment was wrong when he made the trade. This experience drilled into him both the advantage and the necessity of cutting losses short and taught him a lesson he has never forgotten, although, like everyone else, he occasionally departs from his customary practice.

"What I try to do," said he, in explaining to me his methods, "is to make my original commitment as close as I can to the danger point. After making it, I watch to see if that danger point is approached; or I may close the trade out sooner because I think I am wrong; but once the stock moves several points away from the figure where I bought or sold it, I pay little attention to it until it is time to close the trade."

HOW HE LIMITS HIS RISK

He seldom risks more than a few points, which means that the closer to the danger point he can start his operation, the less he ventures. Dealing in large lots of stocks, he cannot slip in and out of the market as easily as a small trader whose hundred share lots are unnoticeable in the transactions of the moment. If what he calls his danger point be 50, he would begin somewhere between that figure and, say, 55. He cannot, like a small trader, place a stop order or limit his risk to a definite figure; but if he sees that his original judgment was in error, he will either sell at the market or wait for a strong spot on which to close out his line.

The relation between the amount of his theoretical risk and the size of his minimum anticipated profit, is a very interesting point and one which most of the public seems to overlook. Operating in stocks being a business or a profession in which a series of transactions results in a certain percentage of losses and profits, it is the operator's purpose to have these profits exceed losses after payment of all expenses incidental to the business. It is for this reason, Mr. Livermore tells me, that he never makes a trade unless he sees at least a probable ten points profit. Of course, many of his profits are much larger than this. I have stated one instance where his profits on a large line ran into fifty points, compared with the few points which he risked on the original trade. But in setting a minimum of ten points as his objective, it will be seen that he is leaving room for one or two losses out of three trades, without extinguishing all the profit he endeavors to secure on the third trade.

I do not mean by this that he is an active trader, for as I have explained, he usually takes a position and waits for an important swing. If he does not get it and the stock does not respond to the influences which should be effective, he concludes that he has made an error, either as to the stock or its direction, or the time at which the trade should be made. The point is that he usually makes a practice of cutting his losses according to the well-tried rule, and when a stock does move in his favor he lets his profit run until, in many instances, it reaches sizeable proportions. The ratio of profit, measured in points, is therefore greater than ten to three or ten to five. The original risk on a trade may have been, say, four points, although it may show a profit of twenty points—a ratio of two to ten—or even more than that.

Like everyone else, he has certain periods wherein his judgment is below par and he is obliged to take frequent losses; otherwise he would be the most successful operator of all times; but as he is, after all, only human, with judgment highly developed but not infallible, he treats such transactions as part of the day's work and strives to have them few enough to yield a positive balance on the ledger.

Take the methods followed by any successful operator, turn them inside out, and you will learn why the public in general is unsuccessful. The public will usually take three points profit and stand for a ten-point loss. Livermore takes a three-point loss and plays for a ten-point profit. A loss of three or four points to him means danger. To the public, it usually means a healthy reaction—nothing to be alarmed at. The public regards a ten-point profit as something seldom attained because unsophisticated traders, if they buy a stock right, have not the patience to hold on that long. To Livermore, a ten-point profit is confirmation of the fact that his judgment in the first instance was correct and that the stock is now beginning to move his way.

One of the simplest rules and at the same time one of the hardest to learn, is this practice of cutting losses short. If everyone who trades in stocks would systematically close out his losing trades once a day, once a week, or once a month, or at a time when a certain number of points loss are indicated, the way would be paved to his success in trading, provided he has the patience to hold on for a substantial profit when a stock does go his way.

These two rules are probably the most important keys to the success not only of Mr. Livermore, but of every other big operator whose dealings have attained the spectacular.

CHAPTER 6

How He Keeps His Capital Turning Over

Having shown how Mr. Livermore closes out a trade when it reaches what he calls his danger point, or when, contrary to his forecast, it shows signs of running into a loss, we will now consider one of his methods which embodies one of the most vital points in stock trading, although it is generally overlooked by the public. I refer to his practice of cutting out trades that do not move in the anticipated direction within a few days, or perhaps a further reasonable time.

Being constantly on the lookout for trading opportunities in which he can risk a comparatively small number of points in an endeavor to secure a liberal profit, he watches the tape for the psychological moment at which the trade may best be made. He may especially have observed a certain stock for many days or weeks, while it was working into a position which he regarded as inviting a trade. The stock may be through with its period of preparation so that now there is no longer any doubt in his mind that it is ready to work in a certain direction. He waits until he is sure he is right. If the stock is being accumulated, he endeavors to secure it on one of the last drives. Its previous gyrations having led him to expect a certain action under given market conditions, he watches it to see that the favorable symptoms do not change.

Suppose it is an oil stock and he has estimated that it is approaching the point where it is ready for a sharp run-up. The other oil stocks indicate strength. This one which he has chosen above others, instead of responding to the upward tendency, shows an inclination to lag. His deduction is that although his prognosis favored a rise, something evidently has developed which may postpone the plans of the insiders or other interests operating in that stock. It may be some bit of news which will cause a temporary decline in price; therefore, instead of being allowed to follow the rest of the oil stocks, support is withdrawn from that issue and it is allowed to sell off. The object may be reaccumulation at a lower level but that makes no difference to him. The stock has had the opportunity to demonstrate its strength or weakness, and when the latter appears he closes out quickly on the ground that he cannot afford to lug along a stock that is not acting exactly according to his forecast. The stock does not necessarily have to show a paper loss; it may be a point or two in his favor when these weak symptoms develop. He closes out when it does not act right, regardless of whether the trade is even, a little above or a little below where he entered it.

"DRIFTING" STOCKS COST MONEY

Of all the trades that eat up an operator's working capital, those stocks that drift around and refuse promptly to go in the desired way, are probably the most destructive. When an operator makes a losing trade and closes it out, he knows definitely what his loss is. But when he allows it to stand, in the hope that within a day or two it will show a more definite tendency and give more promise of profit, then the operator is merely hoping that it will come out all right; and as Livermore says, "When I have to depend on hope in a trade, I get out of it because it will only bother me in my trading and I cannot afford to be on anything but live ones."

In brief: when he buys, he considers that stock a purchase at that time. If he is right, it should advance. If it does not, he knows he is wrong and something has happened to contradict the indications previously given by the stock. In that case he would rather be out.

Everyone with reasonably long trading experience knows that some of his greatest losses have grown out of the trades which were carried along on hope. In this class come all the securities which were "bought on put away." Some people think when a stock or a bond is deposited in the strong box, it is safe. It may be safe from fire and theft, but it is never immune from shrinkage in market value.

Keeping the trading capital in proper circulation is a sound principle in Wall Street as well as in merchandising. Suppose these great department stores on Fifth Avenue failed to put their slow moving goods on the bargain counters and clean them out; soon they would find their liquid capital shrinking, much of it tied up in undesirable merchandise—gathering dust on the counters and in the store-rooms. They could not stay in business. But let one of these merchants go into the security market and he will abandon the principles which have made his department store a success. He will buy a stock, take a small profit, buy another and carry it along, especially if it shows a loss, until it goes ten, twenty or thirty points against him, causing not only a shrinkage in his capital, but something more important—

something that few people realize. I refer to the *opportunities* which are lost by reason of the carrying of these unprofitable trades.

Every merchant and manufacturer endeavors to turn over his capital as many times as he can during the year; but if part of his capital is frozen then only what remains can be turned over, and his net profit for the period is, as a result, far below what it should have been because he has been obliged to miss many chances to purchase desirable goods at attractive prices, and thus have been enabled to turn over his *entire* working capital. It is such a situation that Mr. Livermore is very careful to avoid. He aims to take advantage of the cream of the opportunities that come along from time to time; to get in the right stocks at the right time and ride them in the right direction. Hence, he clears out the deadwood just as an expert bowler wants the pin boy to take away the pins that he has knocked down but are still lying among those standing.

WHY HE'S ALWAYS READY FOR OPPORTUNITIES

Every year or two there is a great opportunity either to accumulate a big line of stocks at the bottom of a panic or heavy decline, or to sell short a considerable line at the high levels of a boom. If Mr. Livermore were long or short of a lot of trades that he had been *hoping* would come out all right sooner or later, his judgment would not be so clear at these vital spots in the market, when his most important undertakings are entered into.

Combined with his rule of cutting losses short, the above described practice gives him both a limit as to the *amount* of his risk and the *period of time* in which he will devote working capital in an attempt to make money out of any particular trade. Thus, he has both a *price* stop and a *time* stop.

He will not stay with a trade more than a few points if his judgment appears to be wrong as to its direction, and he will not stay with it more than a few days if it does not perform as it should within that time.

These two methods are what might be called the lifeblood of his trading methods, because they keep his capital in constant circulation and enable him instantly to command it for the market opportunity which is most promising at a given moment.

CHAPTER 7

The Kind of Stocks In Which To Trade

We have shown how Mr. Livermore does not make a commitment unless it promises to yield his minimum anticipated profit; also how he keeps his desk clear of stocks that do not move as and when he expects. Let us now consider the class of stocks in which he deals.

It is obvious that if he is to realize at least a ten-point profit, he cannot devote attention or capital to dealing in stocks which most of the time fluctuate over a narrow range. To be sure, these issues do have ten-point swings, but they are generally many months in accomplishing such movements and do not afford the opportunities for profit that may be had in more volatile stocks; but generally speaking, his method of operating eliminates this blue chip class of stocks except under peculiarly promising conditions. He prefers to deal in the fast movers; stocks that have wide swings—the market leaders. These are usually the best stocks in the most active groups—the ones which will swing fastest and farthest. It is from these that he derives his greatest profits.

I do not mean that any stock is taboo with him so long as he can see the possibilities of a return which is large in proportion to the amount of his risk. He has made considerable money in some of the very low priced issues, and when all is considered, this kind of money is very satisfactory. If a stock purchased at 10 rises to 20, that is 100% on the money involved; whereas a high priced stock would have to rise from 200 to 400 to make the equivalent. There is a vast difference, however, in the number of points traveled by a stock from 10 to 20 compared with a high priced stock moving from 200 to 400, and it is the large number of *points* that he is after.

In the case of a stock selling at 10, he would naturally buy it outright so that his risk would be ten points, or whatever amount less than that he chooses to cut his loss if an adverse movement should set in. When trading on the long side of a high priced stock, however, he probably would not carry this if he bought at 200 and it went several points against him, because his indications for a rise would doubtless be nullified should the stock recede to 193 or to 190 after he had purchased it. All of this depends, of course, upon the character of the market and the action of the stock and other stocks in that group at the time. As we have said, each stock market picture is a different one and has to be judged on its own merits. Operating as he does there is no such increase in percentage of risk as between the $10 stock and the $200 one as might be indicated by the difference in price; but the real incentive in the higher priced stock is the large number of points, which means that profits run into big figures when a round lot of stock is purchased and his judgment proves correct.

Livermore has said: "Stick to the strong industries and pick out the strongest securities in those industries."

Of course, he is not married to any particular kind of stock, but trading in round lots and expecting quick responses and wide swings, his selection is more circumscribed than that of the average man whose trading makes little or no impression on the tape; nor is he in exactly the same position as those operating what are known in Wall Street as the banking pools, whose operations are so large and conducted over such periods of time that they require a ten-point range in which to accumulate a line of stocks and another ten-point range for distribution. As a rule he can succeed in getting the greater part of his line within a range of a few points unless circumstances require haste. His operations usually being spread over a number of stocks, they do not require him to swing an unwieldy line of any one issue for his own individual account, but in his operations as manager of a number of stock market pools these might run into several hundred thousand shares.

LIVERMORE WANTS "ACTION" STOCKS

To sum up, what he wants is action—prompt action, combined with a broad market.

There is a lesson in this for those who would be successful in their stock trading: the selection of proper trading mediums is an important consideration. Combined with the other valuable rules formulated as a result of Mr. Livermore's past experience, the reader should by this time have a clear idea of some of the factors which make for success in this business.

Many of the readers will doubtless say to themselves, "that is all very well for Mr. Livermore, but I have a somewhat different idea." You may have, but considering the composite experience of most members of that great faction known as the public, the writer's advice to those who *think* they know more about it than Livermore or any one else, is simply this: forget what you know or think you know about trading in stocks, and apply these rules. In the end you will be far better off than if you persist in sticking to your own imperfect ideas about this very complicated task—one which has taken most of the big and successful operators many years to cut their eye-teeth.

CHAPTER 8

Livermore's Method of Pyramiding

Earlier in this book I referred to some points in the operating methods of Jesse L. Livermore which might be compared to those of the late James R. Keene. One of these is the way in which, many times in the past, Livermore has made a small amount of working capital produce a very large profit.

In the early '90's, Keene had the handling of a pool in National Cordage. It was during the unhealthy markets which preceded the 1893 panic. He ran Cordage up as high as he could, and the whole pool collapsed, carrying with it practically all of the large fortune which Keene had amassed up to that time. When the wreck was cleared away, he had only $30,000, and with this he started to build up a fresh pile of millions.

A well-known newspaper man came to him one day and gave him some information to the effect that one of the Jersey Central's subsidiaries (I believe it was the Lehigh & Wilkesbarre Coal Co.) was in financial difficulties and the result would be very serious for Jersey Central, the stock of which was then selling around 70. Whether this was a trap to catch the old man short, I do not know, but it looked suspiciously like it. Keene began pounding away at the stock and urging other holders to liquidate, but he found strong support at just about that level. After he had almost exhausted his efforts on the short side, the stock began to move up, and by the time it reached 80 he realized that he was wrong, so he switched and took the long side.

He had a big loss and his $30,000 was therefore greatly impaired, but this did not discourage him. He bought all he could and as the stock continued to advance, he increased his line. The rise amounted to about one hundred points from where he started to sell it short, but by that time Keene's $30,000 original working capital had grown into $1,700,000, which put him back on his feet.

In December 1906, Mr. Livermore saw the possibilities on the short side, saw the break coming as clearly as could be, and put out a moderate short line. Every point decline in the stocks he sold gave him that much more leeway, and he promptly took advantage. He kept on selling just as fast as his broker would permit and by the time the first section of the 1907 panic took place—that is, within a few months after he had begun to operate on the short side—he had $1,000,000 to his credit.

A LESSON FROM A COMMODITY SPECULATOR

Pyramiding was nothing new for Livermore in 1907, and although he has since modified his methods in certain particulars, he has not by any means lost the faculty of pressing his advantage. In so doing, he has taken a leaf out of the book of Dickson G. Watts, a very successful cotton operator of a generation ago, who said: "It is better to average up (pyramid) than to average down. This opinion is contrary to the one commonly held and acted upon, it being the practice to buy and on a decline buy more. This reduces the average. Probably four times out of five this method will result in striking a reaction in the market that will prevent loss, but the fifth time, meeting with permanently declining market, the operator loses his head and closes out, making a heavy loss—a loss so great as to bring complete demoralization—often ruin. But buying up is the reverse of the method just explained; that is to say, buying at first moderately and, as the market advances, adding slowly and cautiously to the line. This is a way of speculating that requires great care and watchfulness."

Of course, Mr. Watts did not originate this method, which is as old as Wall Street. Many big speculative fortunes can be traced to it. Addison Cammack used to say, "The Lord is on the side of the heaviest battalions," and he, a famous bear, used to pyramid, pounding prices harder and harder as they went his way.

About eighteen months ago, I was discussing with Mr. Livermore the advantages of pyramiding. I told him that I had seen some wonderful results worked out by this method and with the employment of a very small amount of money. While at that time he was rather inclined to favor the taking of a definite position with the full amount of stock at the original buying or selling level, he has since modified this procedure, so that to a certain extent, we will say for the first several points of a move, he does what might be called limited pyramiding. He now believes that the most enlightened way of following this important practice is, first, to take on part of his line, then as the market confirms the accuracy of his opinion, double up, and if a further favorable action is recorded on the tape, he will complete his commitment. As he operates in substantial lines of stock, his purchases naturally supply an auxiliary impulse in the desired direction.

A COOL HEAD FOR SUPREME DECISIONS

There is another rule of Watts' which Mr. Livermore has adapted with very great advantage, which is: "The fundamental principle that lies at the base of all speculation is this: act so as to keep the mind clear, its judgment trustworthy. A reserve force should, therefore, be maintained and kept for supreme moments, when the full strength of the whole man should be put on the stroke delivered." It is these supreme moments, both at the apex of big bull markets and at the low points of the panics for many years past that Livermore has done his most effective work, for he strongly realizes the immense advantage of covering a big short line and going long when the market is in a state of panic, and of getting out of his longs and going short while the market is boiling on the up side. I do not mean that he has invariably chosen the psychological moment, but his average percentage of accuracy in this respect has doubtless been higher than that of any other leading individual operator for many years past, for it is at such points that the full force of his pyramiding or his patient long swing operations are brought to a climax and a position taken which puts him in line for the next big swing in the opposite direction.

This playing for position is a good deal like laying the foundation for the erection of a building—the more deeply one gets down into the bedrock, the more solid and substantial his structure. In so playing for position when he is operating on the bear side, he must be keenly alive to the possibilities of a reverse movement and be on the lookout for the real buying opportunity. It is from this point, if correctly located, that his pyramiding operations may be begun with the greatest possibility of success. His experience proves that, as a rule, it is not wise to extend pyramids far from their base, for thus the average price of his commitment is such that an important reaction may throw the transaction into a heavy paper loss. This is the basis of his favoring a limited pyramid.

IN SUMMARY

What interests me most in this interview is that Mr. Livermore, with a natural and developed genius for reading the tape, made his success in buying and selling securities only after he became a spec-vestor. His principal operations are conducted just as are those of a merchant who, accurately foreseeing future demand for certain goods, purchases his line and patiently awaits the time when he may realize a profit. Just as legitimately, when he foresees an oversupply, he contracts to deliver in future goods which he believes will then be purchasable at lower prices. Mr. Livermore says: 'There is no magic about success. No man can succeed unless he acquires a fundamental knowledge of economics and conditions of every sort."

The outstanding value of these Livermore experiences is that it shows the average business man, with whom investment and spec-vestment is necessarily a side line, that one need not be a genius to make stock market money.

While few people are by nature gifted to become great operators, a knowledge of Mr. Livermore's methods prove that the best results may be obtained, not by active trading, but by a careful study of the factors which influence the market and business conditions.